I0788764

Dear Customer:
This coloring book presents more that 30 illustrations representing Spring . These illustrations are designed to enhance your skill developing the realistic image. This is not a how-to-color book. This is a coloring book for advanced shading.
~Color realistic images
   You will notice breaks in the line drawing to show where light is reflecting. This extra shading will improve your final picture
~Check out the other coloring books in this series for hours of fun and learning
~Thank you for buying this coloring book please leave a review on Amazon

This Book Belongs to

____

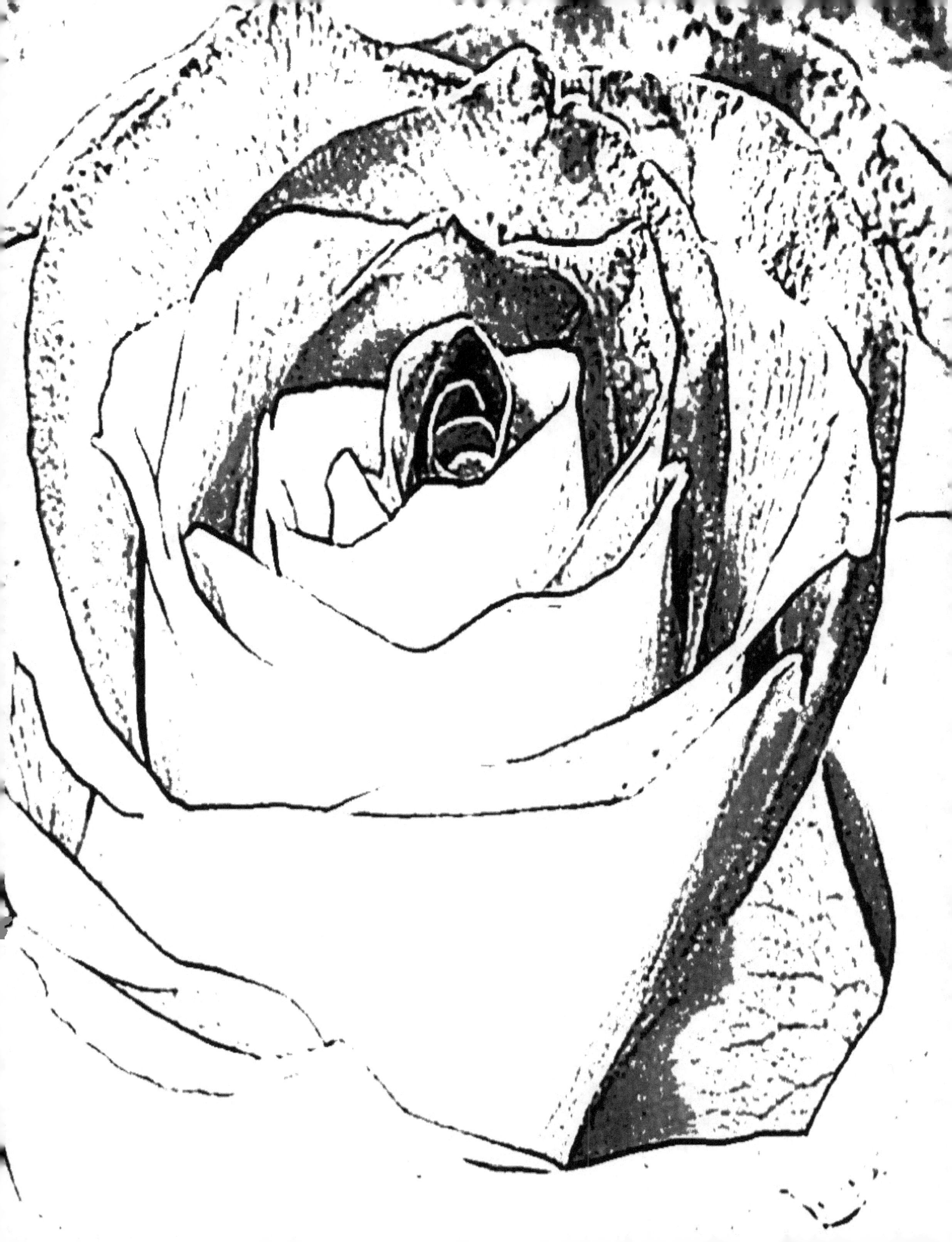

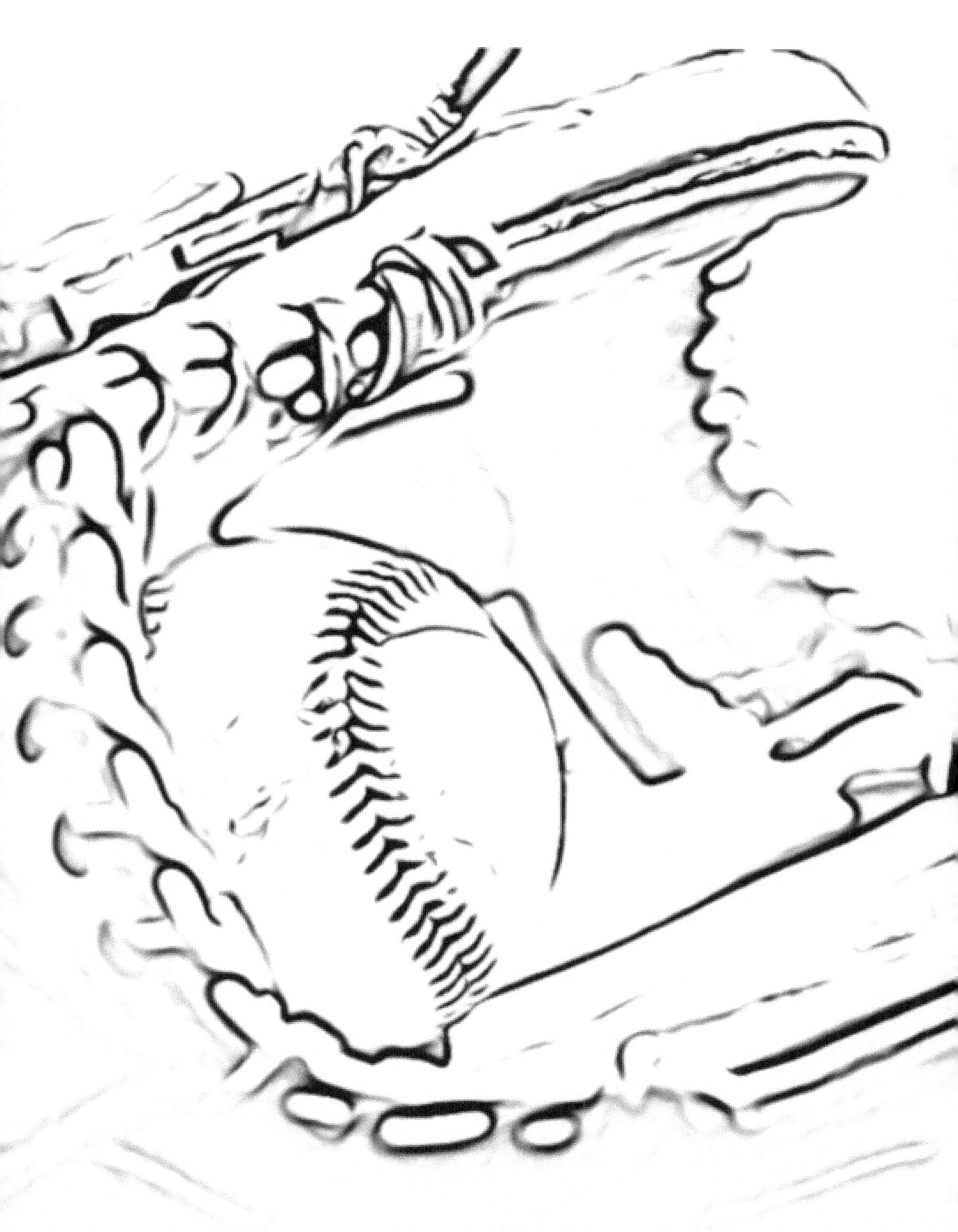

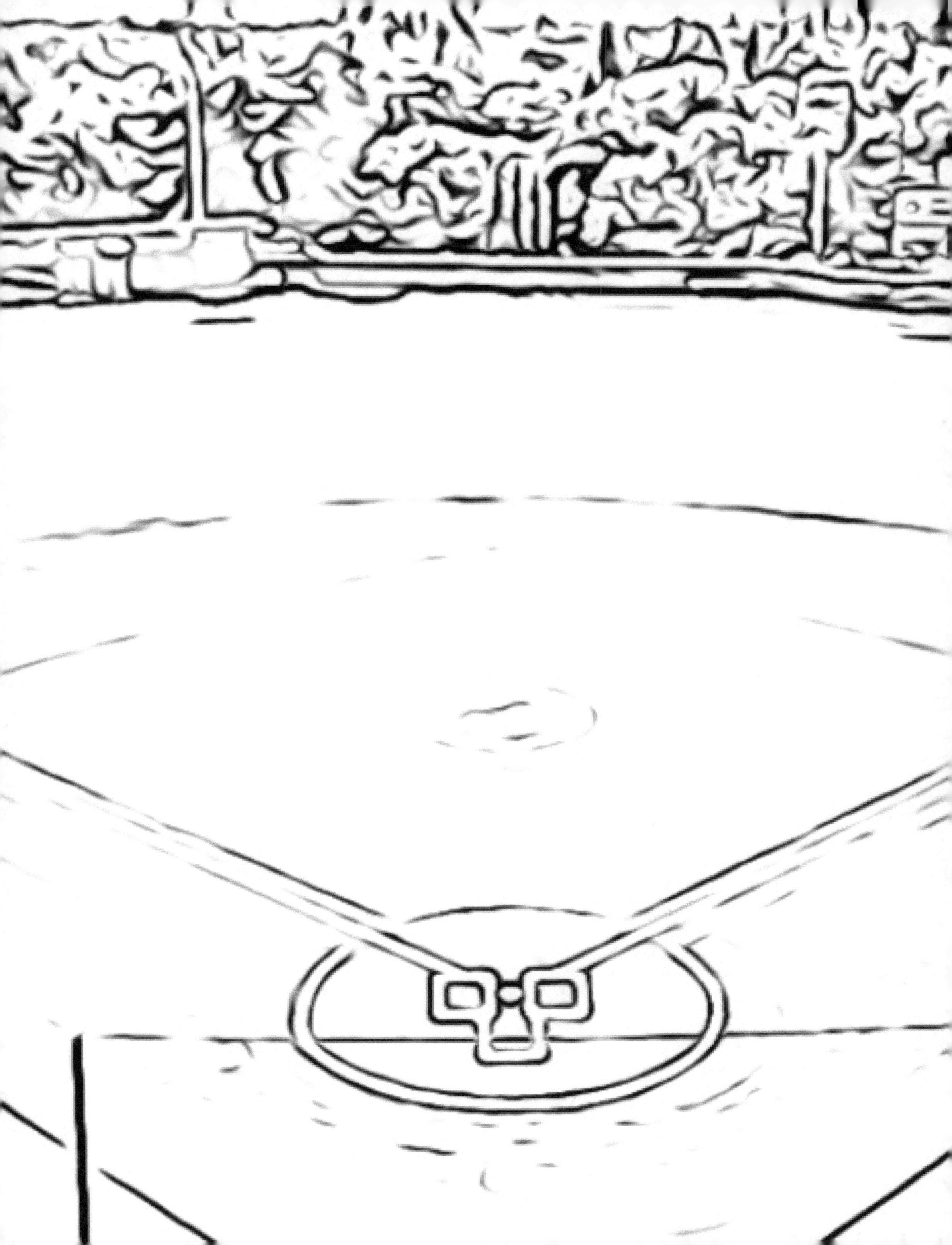

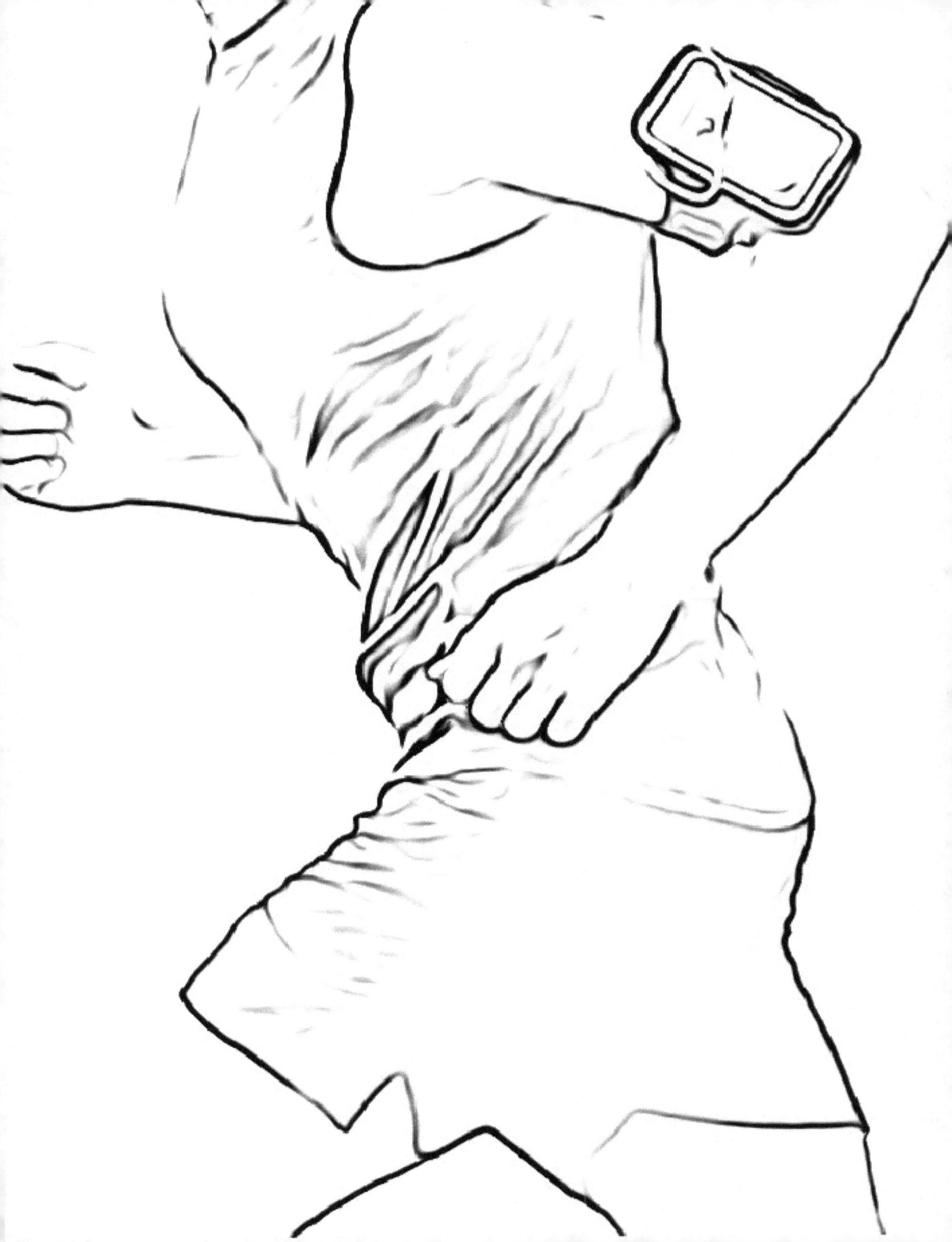

~Check out the other coloring books in this series for hours of fun and learning:
COLORING BOOK: Classic American Truck
~Thank you for buying this coloring book please leave a review on Amazon